justice

VIRTUES OF MY HEART

Written and Illustrated by Melissa López Charepoo

Text and Illustrations
© 2020 Melissa López Charepoo

First published 2020. Reprint 2026.

ISBN 978-1-971750-23-1 (paperback)

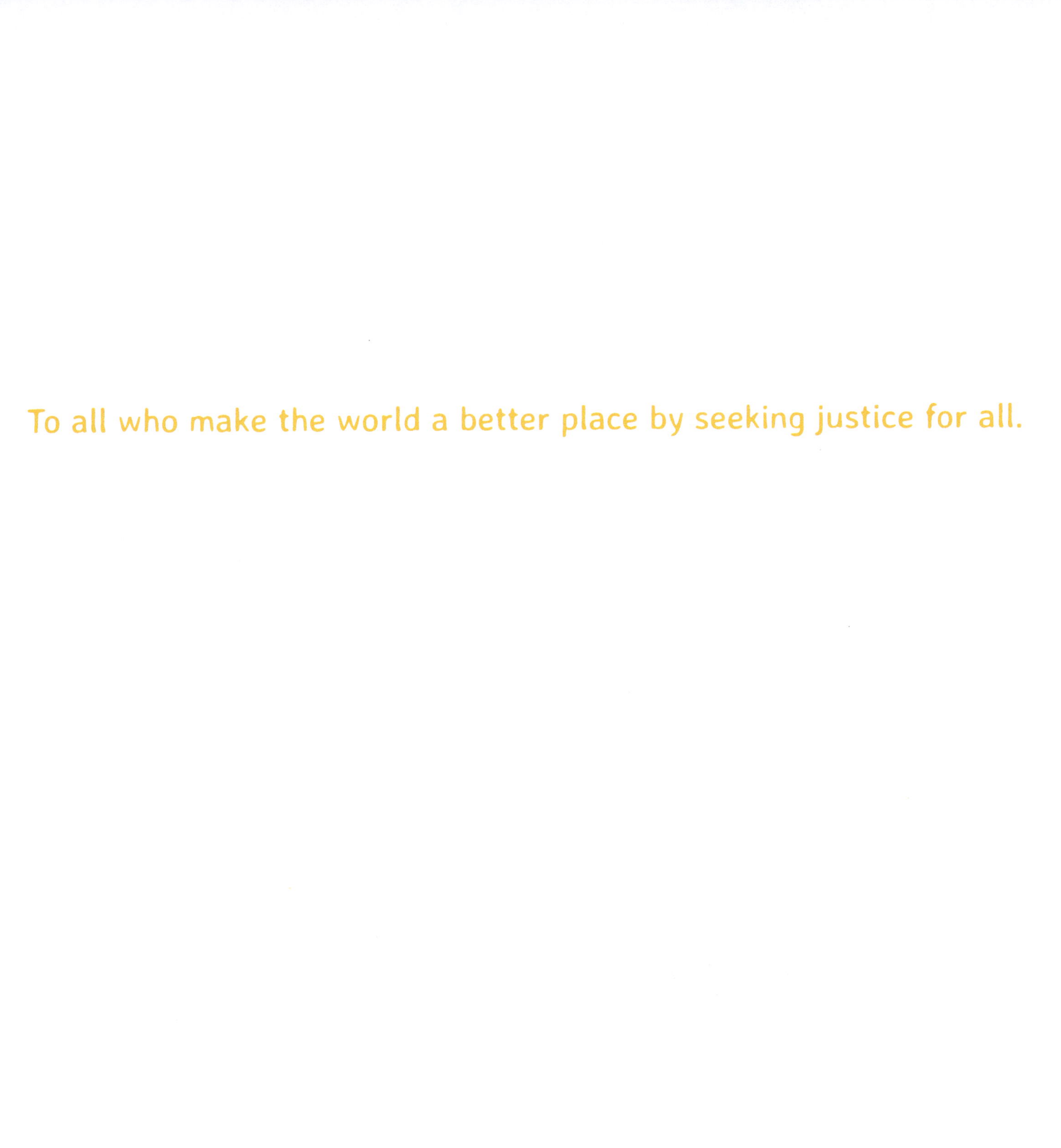
To all who make the world a better place by seeking justice for all.

Have you ever wondered what the word **justice** means?

Justice is being fair in everything we do. It is a virtue, or a good quality of our hearts. We can strive for justice in two ways: as individuals and as society. We strive for justice as individuals by recognizing the nobility of every human being. We strive for justice as a society by standing up for our rights, fulfilling our responsibilities as citizens, and by making sure our society is fair for everyone.

We can strive for justice in everything we do!

As an individual, I practice justice by acting with **independence**. I can think for myself, and I am not convinced solely by the opinions of others. I investigate the truth and form an opinion based on the facts I see.

How do you strive for justice by practicing **independence**?

One way I strive for justice at home is by always being **truthful** to my family. I look to see the truth in any situation I am involved in. I always speak honestly and take responsibility for my actions when I am at fault.

How do you strive for justice by practicing **truthfulness**?

As a friend, I strive for justice by acting with **purity**. I avoid gossiping about others, and I free my heart from all kinds of prejudices. Prejudice is an opinion of an individual, group, or race that in not based in truth. For example, we can have prejudices of skin color, religion, culture, gender, age, and many more. They negatively affect our opinions of others. Having a pure heart, free from prejudice, allows us to see nobility in everyone.

Have you ever experienced prejudice? How do you seek justice by acting with **purity** as a friend?

I seek to resolve issues with my friends. When I have a difference of opinion with others or I feel hurt, I strive for justice by being **assertive**. I also act with **humility** when I listen to other people's perspectives and admit when I have done wrong. I always strive to make amends.

How do you strive for justice by being **assertive** and acting with **humility**?

As part of a community, during sports or at school, I strive for justice by acting with **integrity**. I stand for what I believe is right. I also stand with other people when they face unjust situations.

How do you strive for justice by acting with **integrity**?

In a fair society, justice centers around reward and punishment based in the law. Laws are rules set in society to protect everyone. We are rewarded when we do the right thing. We are punished when we do the wrong thing. In a just society the rewards and punishments are the same for everyone. We act with **wisdom** when we choose to do the right thing by being **obedient** to the law and ensuring that the laws are fair and applied equally to everyone.

What are some of the laws in your society? How do you strive for justice by practicing **wisdom**?

LOVE
JUSTICE
UNITY
WE ARE ONE

Our society can be unfair to an individual or a group of people. We show **empathy** to our fellow citizens when we listen to their experiences and identify things in our society that are unjust to others. By freeing our hearts from prejudices, we have the **courage** to stand for change. Together we can build a more just and fair society for all.

How do you strive for justice by showing **empathy** to those who do not have the same privileges and opportunities that you do? How do you help build a more just society by having the **courage** to stand for change?

As a citizen of the world, I understand that every human being deserves a just and fair society. We must first achieve a just society in order to have **unity**. Only when everyone is treated equally and fairly will harmony and peace appear in the world.

How do you strive for justice as a citizen of the world in order to achieve **unity**?

As you can see, there are many ways that we can strive for **justice** in our daily lives as individuals and as part of society. By practicing justice, we also develop other virtues, such as independence, truthfulness, purity, assertiveness, humility, integrity, responsibility, obedience, empathy, courage, and unity.

Our hearts will always be joyful when we are fair to others and ourselves and when we have the courage to stand for change in creating a more fair and just society!

Glossary

Assertiveness – confident behavior

Courage – the ability to do something that scares us

Empathy - the ability to understand and share the feelings of another

Humility – being humble, modest, and unpretentious

Integrity – the quality of being honest and have strong moral principles

Justice - being fair in everything we do

Obedience - compliance with an order, request, or law

Purity – free from contamination

Truthfulness – honesty, the fact of being true

Unity – being part of a whole; togetherness

Virtue – behavior showing high moral standards; good qualities of our hearts

Wisdom – having good judgment

References:

The Virtues Project Cards
Oxford English Dictionary

Heartfelt thanks to:

My beloved husband Darioush Charepoo for all his support.
Our dearly loved boys for being the inspiration.
Sharon Slocum Greer for helping with proofreading.
Leanna Guillén Mora for helping with proofreading and editing the book.

www.ingramcontent.com/pod-product-compliance
Lightning Source LLC
Chambersburg PA
CBHW042159030726
47599CB00004B/793